T0012210

Reset Your Creativity
Workbook

JESSIE KWAK

art by
NALISHA RANGEL

INTRODUCTION

I stared at the blank page in front of me, a purple crayon in my hand, willing myself to draw something. *Anything*. But forcing it wasn't working. My creative mind was as blank as the paper in front of me.

Meanwhile, my niece had filled her page with a kaleidoscope of reds, yellows, and blacks in a vaguely avian form. She told us it was an eagle; we later dubbed it the Chainsaw Chicken because of its serrated wings and angry-looking beak.

It was wild. Delightful. An image fully formed from the raw creative stuff of her seven-year-old mind.

And my page was still blank.

I stared at her as she grabbed another blank page and uncapped another marker, mystified.

This kid only had seven years of limited experience to draw on, and her imagination was endless. I had almost forty years, and I couldn't think of a single thing to draw.

Where had my own creativity gone?

If you picked up this workbook, I'm going to make the wild assumption that you're struggling, creatively. Maybe you hit a wall, maybe you're overwhelmed and burnt out, maybe you've had your own "blank page" moment where it felt like the thing that used to bring you joy—your creativity—has completely evaporated like a puddle in the desert.

Despite all the ways creativity is used as a buzzword in modern society, when we try to actually *be* creative we find the decks are stacked against us.

Work, family, *adulting*—every task, chore, and worry takes time out of your day. Worse, they each levy a tax on your creativity stores. That's why, even when you manage to clear away time in your day for your art or writing, you end up feeling completely tapped out.

There are lots of books out there that offer ideas for getting the creative juices flowing, and I'll refer to many of them throughout this guide.

My intention here isn't to help distract you and get you feeling playful for a minute, though you'll find a number of suggestions for tapping into your inner seven-year-old, as well as some gorgeous coloring book pages designed by artist Nalisha Rangel for you to print out and color.

Instead, the goal of this book is to help you address the root of the problem, swiftly and powerfully. At the end, you should walk away with increased clarity about what's keeping you from living a more creative life, and a plan to start living it.

This is a program you can come back to anytime you start to feel frazzled, or like you're struggling to tap into your creativity again.

Though the steps remain the same, each time, your answers to the prompts will tailor them to what you need in that specific moment.

HOW TO USE THIS GUIDE

Step 1: Block off thirty minutes a day for the next five days

The time of day doesn't matter—the important thing is to choose a time when you know you'll be uninterrupted. Maybe it's getting up 30 minutes early to work while the house is quiet, maybe it's starting your nighttime routine thirty minutes early to journal before bed, maybe it's blocking out time on your lunch break or commute.

Or maybe it's a combination of all these!

Whatever it is, pull out your calendar and schedule the time right now.

Step 2: Choose where you'll work

Writing longhand in a notebook, typing, dictating—choose where you'll answer the prompts over the next five days. And, hey, if you want to use this as an excuse to buy a gorgeous new journal, be my guest. I'm certainly guilty!

Step 3: Commit to being honest and curious

Wherever and whenever you're writing, commit to answering the questions honestly and curiously. You're the only person who needs to see what you write, so you're only shooting yourself in the foot if you don't tap into your truth.

My goal in this guide isn't just to help you organize the chaos of your life into something manageable, but to provide a legitimate turning point for you when it comes to pursuing your creative goals.

Turning points aren't easy, and they don't generally happen over the course of five days.

So, please be gentle with yourself. Be open. Be curious.

And please reach out to someone (a friend or a professional therapist) if these journaling prompts bring up things you need to discuss more.

Step 4: Recruit a buddy

Speaking of reaching out, this might be a good time to ask a friend if they want to go on this creative reset journey along with you. This is a good way to share your insights and give each other encouragement and accountability as you commit to prioritizing your creativity.

You've got this.

Note: This workbook is meant to be used on its own, but if you want to go deeper I recommend checking out my book From Chaos to Creativity.

Part 1:
Creative Reset

DAY 1: WHAT DO I WANT?

If you're feeling creative burnout, chances are there's something deeper beneath the surface. And you're definitely not alone. The last few years have forced a magnifying glass on some of the shadows below the surface of our society, culture, and day-to-day lives, and a lot of us are rethinking what we want.

That's showing up in our personal lives. I'm grateful that my husband and my relationship has weathered those exposed shadows and gotten stronger, but I know other couples who broke up.

That's showing up in our work. I recently met a woman who'd just quit her career as a teacher, mid-year. "I resigned effective at the end of the month," she said, and the tension in her shoulders disappeared at the words. She grinned. "I don't know what I want to do next, but the pandemic taught me that I didn't want to be a teacher any more."

There are a few ways of asking what you want. You could dream about the creative projects you want to do this year.

Maybe you want to:

- Build up enough paintings to have a show
- Write your first book
- Take up a new hobby
- Start a business

I still want you to think about that.

But I also want you to think about something deeper.

Maybe you're excellent at setting creative goals and running yourself into manic exhaustion (and eventually collapse) to reach them. Stacking more goals on an unexamined foundation isn't going to help you achieve them. It's not going to ease you out of creative burnout.

That's why today we're going to examine the entire foundation of our creative work.

Set aside thirty minutes and journal on this question: *What do I want?*

I know.

This is a much more challenging question to answer than "What creative projects do I want to do next year?"

Asking yourself what you want is a fundamentally selfish question, and many of us were conditioned to put others first at all costs.

I want you to be selfish today.

(For a few minutes, at least. It's a practice, and we'll keep building this muscle over the course of the next five days.)

Ask yourself "What do I want?" Then, keep digging on that question; the answer may have nothing (and everything) to do with your creative work.

For example, when I went through this process, what emerged was that ultimately I want to stop struggling against the expectations (real and imagined) of others so that I can make courageous, Jessie-centered decisions. I realized that the major source of stress for me these past few years isn't the work I've taken on, but the invisible load of expectations and obligations I carry.

That's a very different answer than "I want to publish my new series this year."

"What do I want?" is a question I've been struggling with for months—so if you're just now tuning into that question in your own life, don't expect to answer it today.

But *ask* it.

Try some of these variations to dig deeper:

- What do I want my daily life to look like? Why is that appealing to me?
- Where in my life do I find the most joy? Why am I so lit up in those moments?

- If I could do anything—creative or not—in the next year, what would I do? Why would I choose that?
- What would I do if I had no outside expectations on me? Is there really a reason I couldn't do it now?
- What did I hope I would be doing at this age? Why did I find that so compelling back then, and what elements of that am I doing in my life now?

(Notice the *why* questions in each pair. Keep asking yourself why, like an obnoxious toddler, until you get to the core of truth underneath the surface.)

Try some of these tools to help you focus your thoughts:

- Go for a walk or a hike and let your mind relax before journaling on the question
- Talk it out with a friend or partner
- Meditate for ten or fifteen minutes, then draw or write your response to this prompt
- Try a simple tarot spread for Where you stand now / What you aspire to / How to get there

As a side note: You may not be ready to ask what you want. You may find the answers uncomfortable when they start to emerge from the shadows of your psyche—I certainly can relate.

On the other hand, you may be no stranger to this kind of work, and you're champing at the bit to get to the good stuff in this course.

No matter where you are, if "What do I want" isn't a good prompt for you today, please feel free to spend some time journaling on the creative projects you want to accomplish this year.

The rest of this creative reset will work just as well for you either way.

What do I want?

_____

_____

_____

_____

_____

_____

_____

_____

_____

_____

_____

_____

_____

_____

_____

_____

_____

_____

_____

_____

_____

_____

_____

Once, I tweeted that I was feeling overwhelmed by all the exciting projects I wanted to accomplish. I'd been sketching out my goals for the next year, and just writing down the list exhausted me.

A friend of mine, publisher Ben Gorman, tweeted back:

> *I learned something this year that has helped: the etymology of the verb "decide." It comes from the Latin for "to cut." So when someone asks me to do something or when I have an idea for a new project, I must ask myself:*
>
> *"What would I cut out in order to do this?" Because if I'm not cutting, I'm not really deciding.*

This is not a new concept.

In fact, my husband Robert points out to me all the time that I have to give up something in order to take something else on. But Ben was telling me exactly what I needed to hear at that moment, and his words have stuck in my psyche like a barb ever since.

I want to be able to do it all—is that so big of an ask???

Yeah.

It is.

Yesterday, I asked you to muse on the question, "What do I want?

Today's prompt is, "What will I sacrifice to get it?"

Maybe "sacrifice" isn't a word that resonates with you right now—I like it because it's a word that's big and scary enough to demand we sit up and pay attention before it's too late.

But you could also try:

- What do I need to leave behind to achieve my goals?
- What do I need to cut out of my life?
- What do I need to say no to?

When I've led group creativity practices, I like to ask people to write a No List, which is like a spam filter for your life. It's a list of things like types of projects, social engagements, obligations, etc. that you automatically say no to, and it keeps you from taking on the wrong opportunities. (Because those wrong opportunities prevent you from saying yes to the *right* opportunities later.)

But the problem with a No List is that it's just aspirational until you address your underlying problem. Many of us still say yes to those things. There's some reason we don't truly decide, or cut away, the things that didn't serve us.

When you start asking yourself what you need to sacrifice (leave behind, cut out, say no to), you may notice some non-actionable words coming to the surface:

- Fear
- Comparisonitis
- Perfectionism
- Workaholicism

Those are all great things to stop doing—but they're not *tangible*. The No List is meant to be actionable (I don't take on website copywriting, I don't answer work emails after 5pm.) These words aren't exactly actionable.

But they do have something in common.

When we say yes to something on a No List, it's often because of one of these words. It's because we're coming from a place of comparison and perfection and work stress addiction.

Sure, you may want to say no to agreeing to projects you didn't volunteer for. But what you might really need is to sacrifice is the fear that causes you to consider them in the first place.

I know—that's a weird way of phrasing it. Why would letting go of fear be considered a sacrifice?

In writing fiction, we like to talk about a character's misbelief. (*Story Genius* by Lisa Cron is a fantastic book to dive into this. Ebook links | Print link)

The misbelief holds a character back—it's the thing that we, the audience, are rooting for them to overcome in order to succeed in the story.

A misbelief is bad, but it actually used to serve the character. Maybe their inability to open up emotionally used to protect them from a bad family situation as a child. Maybe their fear of using magic powers once protected them from persecution.

Maybe their fear of committing to their art protects them from ridicule. From criticism. From finding out they're not good enough. From failure.

We're not characters in a book, but our misbeliefs still stem from a protective impulse—which makes them incredibly hard to sacrifice.

(Want some further reading on misbeliefs in our own lives? I recommend *The Big Leap* by Gay Hendricks Ebook | Print, and *The Way Back to You* by Ian Morgan Cron and Suzanne Stabile Ebook | Print.)

As with Day 1, if asking a question like "What do I need to sacrifice/let go of/cut loose" feels too big at the moment, I encourage you to think about your No List instead. (See next page.)

And, as always, don't forget to reach out to a friend or a professional if you need to talk.

Extra Credit: Your No List

Write down ten things you're going to say no to this year. This could be:

- Specific types of work/projects
- Things you know you should stop doing (checking Twitter in the work day)
- Friend requests or activities
- Emotional labor
- Commitments
- Any other sort of requests

These could be things you won't take on any more—or they could be things you'll quit. For example, maybe a volunteer position you've done for years that has become more of a burden than not.

(Just because you said yes to something before doesn't mean you can't say no now.)

Take it one step further and create a "Don't care about it" list, with things you give yourself permission not to make a priority. For example, I've given myself permission not to care about my front yard one bit. I love my house plants, but outside plants are on their own.

What are you going to say no to this month, so that you can say yes to your art?

What will I let go?

_____

_____

_____

_____

_____

_____

_____

_____

_____

_____

_____

_____

_____

_____

_____

_____

_____

_____

_____

DAY 3: WHAT'S MY SCHEDULE LIKE NOW?

Welcome to Day 3 of your creative reset. It's only going up from here. :)

If you're anything like me, you have eleventy-thousand projects you want to complete. You probably also have day job stuff, family obligations, household management tasks, and a ton of other wonderful and not-so-wonderful things eating up your schedule.

Plus sleep, food consumption, and relaxation—all of which are critically important for a well-functioning brain.

I know. You're already acutely aware that there are only so many hours in a day. How do we make the best of them?

We start by taking stock of what we have to work with.

First: How do you feel about your schedule?

Start gathering qualitative data by journaling about your schedule. Here are some prompts to get you going:

- What's your regular routine like? What would your ideal routine be like?
- When are you at your most creative? When do you slump?
- How do you tend to feel at the beginning of every day? Excited, hopeful, and energetic? Overwhelmed before you even get started?
- How do you tend to feel at the end of your day? Accomplished and satisfied? Exhausted? Content?
- What do you love about your routine? What causes you anxiety or frustration?

Now you have a better idea how your schedule is making you feel—so let's gather some quantitative data about what's actually going on.

Start heat mapping your energy

Not every hour of the day is created equal, particularly when it comes to doing creative work.

You may already have an idea of what your creative rhythm looks like, but if not, I highly recommend going through this heat mapping exercise from Charlie Gilkey.

Print out the heat map, then spend the next five days coloring in the concentric circles of every hour based on your energy levels. You'll start to see patterns emerge.

Knowing your creative rhythms is invaluable information to help you schedule your day. For example, I know I have a couple solid blocks of creative intensity—one in the morning, one in the afternoon. That's when I need to schedule my most thoughtful work.

Answering emails, taking meetings, formatting blog posts—anything that doesn't require intense creative focus is best left to the last hour or so of the day, or done right before lunch when my focus is starting to waver.

(Charlie also has some great tips on how to optimize your creative energy in the post I linked to above.)

Finally: Begin tracking your time

I find tracking my time extremely obnoxious—but I'm always really glad when I do it. It's an eye-opening exercise, in part because we often overestimate or underestimate how long we spend on things.

For example, I put off answering emails yesterday because I thought it would take forever. But looking at my time log for today, I actually only spent 17 minutes on email.

Tracking your time can have the added bonus of keeping you on task, too. After all, if I have to switch my timer from "Writing" to "Twitter" in order to doomscroll, I'm more likely to just keep writing.

You can use a spreadsheet or a print-out if you like, broken down into 15- or 30-minute increments.

(Laura Vanderkam, author of *168 Hours: You Have More Time Than You Think*, has some fantastic templates on her site. You might also want to check out this podcast with Laura for more great advice from the queen of time tracking. If you want to go deeper into time management, I highly recommend Laura Vanderkam's *168 Hours: You Have More Time Than You Think.* (Ebook | Print)

Or, you can use a time-tracking app. I personally love Toggl. It has lots of features available on the free tier, including the ability to assign tasks to different projects, and tag things. It also gives you different views to help you see at a glance where you're spending your time.

You can track every minute, or be a bit more relaxed about throwing time into categories.

(Though, keep in mind that if you're multi-tasking, you're probably not *actually* doing whatever you categorized that time as.)

You don't even have to track every hour if you don't want to.

For example, I decided to stop tracking sleep as a category because I can see at a glance where the big blank block is between the last block of the night and first block of the morning. (And because I was tired of Toggl sending me an email saying "Hey did you know your timer is still running for Sleep?")

I also decided not to track time on the weekends, because I'm deliberately trying to curb my unhealthy workaholic tendencies and take actual days off. Tracking time on that first Saturday spiked my "I should be working" anxiety, so I shut it down.

I decided to color code my projects in a way that would be immediately apparent where I'm spending my time, based on what my priorities are:

- Bright "Go Light" green for fiction work
- Darker green for nonfiction writing
- A pleasant, relaxing teal for time spent with friends, my husband, or relaxing activities
- Healthy bright blue for workouts, and self-improvement
- A sunny yellow for client work
- Cautionary orange for "business of business" admin stuff—it's necessary, but I know I can waste time getting caught up in it
- Warning red for puttering, procrastination, etc
- "Meh" gray for housework and running errands. Gotta be done.

(If you're using Toggl, it's pretty easy to go in and make bulk edits after the fact to help you with your categorizations.)

However you decide to track your time, commit to doing it for at least a week. We'll talk about what to do with all this intel you're gathering in Part 2: Going Deeper.

What's my schedule like now?

_____

_____

_____

_____

_____

_____

_____

_____

_____

_____

_____

_____

_____

_____

_____

_____

_____

_____

_____

_____

_____

DAY 4: WHAT'S MY IDEAL SCHEDULE?

I woke up recently with my to-do list swirling in my head. I had a handful of large projects I was hoping to wrap up by the end of the week, and they were all crashing around inside my brain.

I knew I didn't need to be stressed about them. It would be a lot of work, but I had plenty of time to do it all.

So why couldn't I get my brain to relax?

I finally realized that my brain was scrambling that particular morning because I'd fallen away from my habit of scheduling out my week. Between vacation travel and holiday chaos, I'd just compiled myself a massive to-do list with no rhyme or reason to it.

I figured I'd just sort it out as I went through the week, but my early morning brain didn't see it that way at all. All my brain saw was a toppling tower of obligations.

Panic mode initiated.

Yesterday, I asked you to start tracking your time and monitor your creative energy to get a handle on your schedule.

Today, I want to talk about taking charge of that schedule—because it's tough to make the most of your creative time when you don't feel clear-headed in your day-to-day work.

I go into this much more deeply in my book *From Chaos to Creativity,* but essentially a creativity system planning process has three steps: Capturing the chaos (all your to-dos/projects/etc), setting priorities, and sorting and scheduling the chaos according to your priorities

(Here's a handout that digs into this a bit more.)

We've done some work around your priorities this week, so today, we're going to focus on **setting up your weekly and daily schedule**

Like tracking your time helps you see where it's going, allocating it ahead of time helps you understand how much you can realistically take on.

When I'm diligent about scheduling out my week, I know exactly what needs to happen every day of the week—which makes me more likely to do it even if I don't feel like it.

It also makes it easy for me to say yes or no to a client's project or a friend's invitation. I never have to guess if I'll be too busy because I can instantly see what my priorities are for the next few days and realistically tell whether or not I have time to take it on.

Here's what my schedule template looks like in Evernote:

Monday	Meetings	
	Deadlines	☐
	To Dos	☐
Tuesday	Meetings	
	Deadlines	☐
	To Dos	☐
Wednesday	Meetings	
	Deadlines	☐
	To Dos	☐
Thursday	Meetings	
	Deadlines	☐
	To Dos	☐
	Meetings	
Friday	Deadlines	☐
	To Dos	☐
Maybe...	Next week	

(It's rainbow, of course, because rainbow is my favorite color.)

Because I'm a visual person, I then block out time in a weekly schedule template in my bullet journal. You'll find a printable schedule template for this step on the next page.

WEEK OF: _ _ _ _ _ _ _ _ _ _ _ _ _

	MON	TUES	WED	THURS	FRI	SAT	SUN
7a							
8a							
9a							
10a							
11a							
12p							
1p							
2p							
3p							
4p							
5p							
6p							
7p							

WEEKLY SCHEDULE PLANNING

I set aside a weekly planning session of about 30 minutes either Friday afternoon or Sunday evening to set up my "This Week" note and block out my time for the week. Here's what happens during that session:

- Delete all of the old appointments, deadlines, and to-dos from the note.
- Go through my calendar and add any appointments for the week under Meetings for each day.
- Add in any deadlines for each day under Deadlines.
- Work backward from every deadline and schedule related tasks like "research article" or "draft article" in the To Do section of previous days.
- Go through my email inbox to see if there's anything that needs to be scheduled into Deadlines or To Dos. Things like to follow up with someone, go to an event, whatever.
- Add any other to-do items that need to happen on a specific day, like "send pet fee request to AirBnB guest," or "call sister to say happy birthday."
- Fill in non day-specific to-do items on days that look light.

I also take this time to glance through my "Brain Dump" note and check in with any future projects to see if it's time to start nudging them along.

Next, I translate those to-do list items and deadlines into actual time blocks by filling out my weekly schedule in my bullet journal (or the printable one above.)

I do this in pencil at first, then as I go through the day I fill out what I'm actually doing in pen. (And color code it, because of course I do.)

- Start by blocking out meetings, commute time, and other immobile events. (Example below.)
- Then, block off when you'll work on your biggest priority projects. Aim for larger blocks where you can really dig in and focus.
- Next, add blocks for second-biggest priorities.
- Finally, fill in blocks for admin, etc.

WEEK OF:_____

	MON	TUES	WED	THURS	FRI	SAT	SUN
7a							
8a	Commute	Commute	Commute	Commute	Commute		
9a							
10a	Meeting						
11a							
12p	Lunch	Lunch	Lunch	Lunch	Lunch		
1p		Doctor apt.					
2p				Meeting			
3p							
4p							
5p			Dinner with Friend				
6p							
7p							

If this seems like overkill, you can also just jot down a schedule. For example:

- 9-11a – Work on Project A
- 11a-11:30a – Client call
- 11:30a-12p – Invoicing
- 12p-1p – Lunch/answer emails
- 1p-3p – Work on Project B
- 3p-5p – Work on Project C

The big thing is to get a visual understanding of how many project focus blocks you can fit in each day, and scheduling them with your creative energy.

I tend to have one good work block in the morning, which I reserve for my biggest priority. I can sometimes manage two distinct projects in the afternoon, but I always schedule the one that requires less brain power at the end of the day.

I also schedule time for things that don't need intense focus, like answering emails or invoicing, during times when I know I'll be a bit distracted.

Whether you sketch out a simple schedule like the example above or fill out a weekly time block schedule, put it somewhere you can see it throughout the day.

This helps keep you on track and trust that whatever you're working on in the moment, it's the right time for it.

Your turn!

Take some time today to schedule out the rest of your week. It will probably take a few goes to settle into a planning method that works for you, but don't worry. With experimentation, it will start to gel.

Tomorrow we're going to move on from the nitty-gritty of planning, and talk about the reason you probably picked up this workbook:

Building creativity back into your schedule.

What's my ideal schedule?

_____
_____
_____
_____
_____
_____
_____
_____
_____
_____
_____
_____
_____
_____
_____
_____
_____
_____
_____
_____
_____
_____

I first read Laura Vanderkam's *168 Hours* back when I was working full time as an in-house catalog copywriter.

I remember being incredibly frustrated when she said a lot of the same cutesy things I tossed out in yesterday's exercise, like "schedule your most important work during your best creative time!"

I wasn't an early-morning person, and I had to be out the door by 7am to make it to my job. By the time I got back and had dinner, my brain was fried.

My best creative time was being taken up by someone else's priorities—and I knew I could only spend so many months forcing myself to write a novel on my lunch breaks before I really hated life.

If that resonates with you, you're not alone.

For me, the answer was to go freelance—which came with its own time-crush struggles. It was years before I felt stable enough to make regular time for fiction writing alongside client work. But, eventually, I got there.

I'm not saying that in order to be creative you have to quit your job (although having been a freelancer for the last decade I'm very Team Quit Your Job).

I'm saying that you have to work with the schedule you've got right now—even if you're also working towards something that's more like what you want.

You may have a demanding job you love. You may be dealing with limited energy because of illness or children or family obligations. You may be going through a major life upheaval, and not have the first clue what next week will look like—let alone have the wherewithall to plan projects out months in advance.

We'll talk a bit more about all this in Part 2: Going Deeper. But right now I want to scale way, way down from the big picture.

- You've been thinking about what you want (in a very large sense).
- You've been thinking about what you'll cut out to get it.
- You've been tracking your time and creative energy to see where it goes.
- You've been learning how to sort the chaos of your life into a schedule.

Today, I want you to spend some time journaling about the one SMALL creative habit you could add to that schedule.

What one SMALL step do you want to take every day that will lead you down the path towards your goals?

Here are some ideas—all 30 minutes or less.

Don't overthink it! Just go with your gut.

Morning Pages

Maybe you want to build a regular writing habit. Good news! You've already spent some time this week building one great creative habit: morning pages.

Morning pages are a concept laid out by author Julia Cameron in her book, *The Artist's Way.* (Here's a link to her explanation of them.)

Essentially, it's the practice of sitting down first thing every morning and journaling—writing down whatever comes to mind, without a filter. Just writing, and seeing what bubbles up.

There's no right way to do morning pages. (You don't even have to write them in the morning.) You can use a prompt, like we have for the last few days. Or you can just write—either way, the idea is to be completely honest and open with yourself.

The main rule of morning pages is that they're for *you*. Nothing you write should be meant for an audience.

Write until you get to three pages longhand, or 750 words if you're typing. Keep writing until you hit that mark, even if it feels like you don't have anything left to say. I guarantee the deeper you scratch, the more interesting things you uncover.

Try building a habit of morning pages over the course of the next month, and see how it works for you.

Morning Not-Pages

Maybe journaling isn't your cup of tea; maybe another art form is better suited to helping you center your thoughts.

Take the concept of morning pages—free expression without purpose—into your own art.

Set a timer and spend twenty minutes doodling, playing nonsense melodies on the piano, tearing up paper to explore color and shapes, spilling ink on canvas, snipping pieces of fabric.

The main rule of morning pages still applies: you're not creating work meant for an audience. You're using your medium to tap into *you*.

Set a Tiny Quota

Most of us are doing creative projects that are big and complex. Maybe you're writing a novel, maybe you're learning to paint, maybe you're recording an album.

In the moment, it may not feel like you're making much progress—and you might be tempted to set big goals to make up more ground.

However, setting big goals can quickly become discouraging if life gets in the way.

Stop stressing about reaching your goal quickly, and start thinking about building a creative habit that gets you to the goal in the long term.

For example, commit to spending 10-30 minutes a day on your art. Commit to writing 300 words on your novel.

You can always go past that, but hitting that small goal will give you encouragement.

Go for a Walk

Sometimes, what our creativity needs most is an opportunity to daydream. Go for a walk with no intention but to discover something new.

Maybe it's a new type of plant in a neighbor's yard, maybe it's an alleyway you've never noticed before.

Just let your mind wander as your body does, and notice how that makes you feel.

Meditate

This is the creative habit I've been cultivating recently.

When I'm busy and overwhelmed, I struggle to find the time to meditate. Yet when I meditate regularly, I feel less overwhelmed—even though I spent fifteen minutes sitting on a cushion instead of knocking things off the to-do list.

Like walking, meditation is one of those foundational habits that isn't explicitly creative, but it gives you a good base upon which to build other creative habits.

I use the <u>Calm app</u>, but I've also heard good things about <u>Headspace</u>. Both of them have decent free-tier features.

Get Curious

Keep a list of questions. Things you've always been curious about, questions that come up throughout the day: What kinds of birds live in that tree out back? What the hell was the Prussian empire? How many albums has Willie Nelson released?*

Start each day by picking one of those questions and digging into it for 20-30 minutes.

This can be related to your art, or simply something you've been curious about—the idea is to build the daily habit of exploration.

* Willie Nelson has released 95 studio albums like an absolute monster—including one hilariously titled *The IRS Tapes: Who'll Buy My Memories?*, the profits of which cleared his outstanding $32 million debt to the IRS. Did you know he lived in Portland, OR for his early career? Did you know he claimed to have smoked marijuana on the White House roof, and is a vocal supporter of LGBT rights? Do you know how gorgeous a record *Teatro* is? Do you know why it has taken me so long to write this section?

Moving on.

Play

One of the best things I did at the beginning of the pandemic was to buy a bunch of Sculpey clay and make random things out of it. Like, not even beads or figures—just combining colors, cutting shapes, baking them into tiny rainbow sculptures when I was done.

I was playing with no purpose, and it gave me the outlet I needed to simply let myself relax.

Set a goal to play each day, with no purpose but to unwind and let your mind explore in a creative way.

Grab your kids' LEGOs. Go collect some rocks from the yard and paint them. Make a secret castle out of twigs and mud in your garden. Make a diorama. Dance to your favorite song.

Your turn:

Pick a creative habit you want to form this month, and commit to it.

Write it on a Post-it. Tell your partner, kids, or accountability buddy about it. Go post it on social media or your blog.

And then **update your weekly and daily schedule to include 20-30 minutes for this habit.**

PS: As you're refining your creative habits, I recommend reading *The One Thing* by Gary Keller and Jay Papasan—it's all about finding that one thing you can do every day to most effectively reach your goals. (Ebook | Print)

And here's some highly-recommended further reading on habits:
Better than Before: Mastering the Habits of Our Everyday Lives, by Gretchen Rubin
Atomic Habits by James Clear (Ebook | Print)

What creative habit will I cultivate?

_____

_____

_____

_____

_____

_____

_____

_____

_____

_____

_____

_____

_____

_____

_____

_____

_____

_____

_____

_____

_____

Part 2:

Going Deeper

BONUS 1: GETTING REAL ABOUT YOUR TIME

I asked you to track your time. So, what do you do with this data you've been gathering? However you track your time, schedule 30-60 minutes to look over your logs and do some reflection.

Here are some questions to ask yourself:

What do I love about my time log? (I spent a good amount of time with friends and my husband, and every single night is colored "teal," which means I actually relaxed in the evenings instead of working.)

What was I surprised took so long? (I apparently take a lot longer to make meals and to get rolling in the mornings than I thought.)

What days was I most fulfilled by, and what did they look like? (I was most fulfilled by days where I could focus on one big project rather than bouncing between multiple smaller projects.)

What are your time sucks, and when do they distract you most? (Twitter and Slack; I tend to be most susceptible when my focus is drained. I spent at least an hour messing around Friday morning before finally knuckling down and going to work.)

Where might I experiment? (I'm playing with the types of breaks I take throughout the day, and I've noticed that on days when most of my breaks are red Twitter or Slack sessions, my green focus work blocks tend to be shorter and choppier. On days when I take longer breaks away from the screen—doing art while listening to a podcast, or doing housework or whatever—the focus work blocks tend to be longer, as well.)

If time tracking helps you, keep it up for a few more weeks.

If time tracking gives you more frustration than insight, though, feel free to ditch it. There's no one way to do anything in these here parts—except for the way that makes you happiest and the most fulfilled.

And speaking of being at your happiest and most fulfilled, let's talk about some of the disconnects that might be emerging now that you're really thinking about where your hours go.

One of the big themes that tends to come up when I ask people to do this exercise is day jobs. For most of us, the day job has immobile hours that may conflict with your creative time, and tracking your time can help you realize how little of your own day you actually have control over.

I understand how frustrating it can be to hear things like "just prioritize your creative work during your creative hours" while you're also balancing day job.

I started this course with the question "What do you want" for a reason.

Today let's talk about what you want out of your job.

Real quick: Whatever your obligations are—whether a traditional day job or something else—we all will have chunks of time that aren't ours to control.

I'm specifically talking about day jobs because that's often the biggest thing, but a lot of the following will be relevant to anyone who's struggling to balance other obligations.

What do you want out of your job?

My goal is to help you on a path towards a life where you're more creatively fulfilled—and that can look like many things.

William Carlos Williams is known for his poetry, but spent his career saving lives as a pediatrician. Philip Glass was a plumber and taxi driver even while his music was critically acclaimed. Toni Morrison worked as an editor for Harper Collins for twenty years while her novels were making waves.

Maybe your goal is ultimately to support yourself with your creative work.

That goal comes with its own challenges and pressures—it's tough to enjoy the creative process when you know your next book/painting/song needs to earn X amount in order to keep your bank account in the black.

Maybe your goal is to work in a field that uses your creative skills.

Which also comes with challenges—working in a field that's adjacent to your art can be much harder than one that has nothing to do with it. I wrote a lot more words of fiction during the years that I waited tables than the years I worked as a catalog copywriter—or those early years of freelancing.

Maybe your goal is to work a job you enjoy that enables the rest of your joys in life.

In fact, one of the things I loved about waiting tables was how many of my coworkers at the Elysian were using the job to support their art. I worked with aerial performers. Singers. Graphic designers and painters. Other coworkers were waiting tables because it supported their desire to travel.

Whatever your goal, step one here is to be honest with yourself about your job situation.

I am very much a meditation novice, but one thing that resonates with me every time is when a teacher points out how much of our frustration comes from wishing we were in a different situation, rather than accepting the reality we're in.

Put another way, if you're measuring your happiness against what you *don't have* rather than being aware and curious about what you *do have*, you're missing a huge opportunity and pouring energy into the wrong place.

Spend some time journaling today about your job (or whatever it is that's soaking up your time). Here are some prompts:

- **How do you feel about your job?** Do you hate it? Are you in the right one? Are you fulfilled? Are you looking for something slightly different? What parts would you keep? What parts would you get rid of?
- **How does your job relate to your creative work?** Does it give you time for your art? Resources? The breathing room to relieve the pressure of earning a living from your art, so you can spend time creating work that's important to you, rather than strictly commercial? Is your work creative? Do you want it to be more creative?
- **What are your priorities right now?** What's the most important thing on your plate right now? Taking care of family? Your health? Your day job? Your creative work? They won't all be at the top of the list, and that's okay—there are seasons for everything. Be clear about which priorities are in season at the moment.
- **When it comes to work in general, what lights you up?**

On that last question, I recommend taking <u>Jonathan Fields' Sparketype test</u> (free) to get a sense of this.

His book, *Sparked!* (<u>Ebook</u> | <u>Print</u>) is a fantastic read—it helps you understand what types of work get you in the groove the most, and what other aspects of your personality serve that.

For example, I'm a Maker, through and through. I love creating things, whether that's books, art, clothes, tables to sew those clothes on, dinner, websites, whatever.

My shadow "sparketype" is Maven, which is all about collecting knowledge. I enjoy learning, but I basically only learn in service to what I'm making. For example, I'll spend hours learning enough of a 3D graphics design program to do the one task I need to, then immediately forget how to even open the program. I wish I retained things better, but if that thing isn't immediately useful to my Maker, my brain tosses it right out the window.

Taking the Sparketype test is a great way to get some insight into what's working—or not working—with your day job.

How can you find creative time around your obligations?

Explore some of these ideas to help you integrate your day job/core obligations and your creative work:

- **Ask where your schedule can shift.** Maybe this is impossible. But maybe you can talk with your manager or your team and find areas where you can make your schedule more flexible. Can you come in late once a week? Can you work through lunch and leave early some days? Hopefully you work somewhere that's supportive of you. But maybe—if you're in a position that I was and your boss won't give you any wiggle room—it's time to start seeking out a position that's more in line with the life you want.
- **Take small bites of creativity.** This workbook is all about building creative habits rather than making huge sweeping goals. Set yourself tiny, ten-minute creative goals this week, and schedule them at a different time every day to explore when works best with your schedule. The answer might surprise you.
- **Find your focus.** If you're working around a day job, you simply won't have the bandwidth to do All The Creative Things. Stay laser focused on one project at a time. Finish it and move to the next thing, rather than spending your limited creative time over a bunch of different projects.
- **Organize your creative to-do list by energy.** If you only get one precious two-hour chunk of peak creative time per week, don't spend it on a series of 5-10 minute tasks you could have knocked out while mostly brain dead after dinner. Be mindful of not letting low-energy tasks soak up the high-energy time you have.
- **Rethink how you unwind.** How are you spending your downtime? You need unstructured downtime—you absolutely do. But are you spending it on Twitter or binging shows you're not interested in? Or are you spending it on things that make you feel refreshed and uplifted and creative?
- **Reimagine your constraints.** You may have a non-negotiable 1-hour commute each way, but it doesn't have to be wasted time. I have a friend who dictated the first draft of his first novel while stuck in LA traffic every day. Take a look at the parts of your day that are most frustrating. How could you spin them into a more enjoyable—I dare say *creative*—part of your day?

How can you find balance?

Finally, I want to leave you with the idea of balance.

Finding work-life balance, to me, doesn't mean perfectly allocating the hours of every day. I prefer to think of balance in terms of seasons.

For me, December is always a season of holiday travel and family, which takes priority over my creative work. For years I struggled with the fact that I wasn't meeting my

(ridiculously ambitious) goals, but I'm trying to learn how to relax into vacation. When I do, I often find I can knock out a month's worth of work in two weeks afterwards.

Weird how refilling your creative reserves is actually helpful.

You may be in a season that's skewed towards taking an important step in your career. You may be in a season of art and creativity. You may be in a season of prioritizing relationships, or caretaking, or rebuilding your health.

What season are you in right now?

I'm a huge fan of <u>Fitness Blender's free workout videos</u>.

(Not an affiliate link, I just seriously love them.)

They're easy to do at home, require next to no equipment, and the instructors who lead you through the exercises are super down to earth—there's no blasting pop music and screaming for you to *smile, SMILE, dammit!!*

I've learned some good stuff about exercise technique from Fitness Blender's founders Kelli and Daniel over the years, and one of the biggest lessons they've taught me is to never skip your warmup.

Taking five minutes to warm up before you start lifting weights or doing a HIIT routine makes your actual workout better because it allows you to work harder while reducing the potential for injury. So even on days when I'm feeling rushed, I know that if I only have 30 minutes for a workout, taking five of those minutes to warm up is the smartest thing to do.

If you've been feeling frustrated during your creative sessions I have a question for you.

e you skipping the warm up?

It's easy to do—especially if you only have a limited amount of time to get those words on the screen or paint on the canvas.

Next time you sit down to work, though, set a timer for five minutes and stretch your creative muscles. Play scales, do some quick sketches (the site <u>Quickposes.com</u> is great for fast practice!), freewrite a poem.

Personally, I like to do a quick journaling check-in with myself about whatever project I'm working on, or do a playful brainstorming session around different colors, scents, or sensations my character might be feeling.

Another writer I know likes to start his writing sessions by re-typing passages from authors whose writing he admires. It primes his writing muscles to get in the flow of good prose.

When I talk about the warm up, I'm not just talking about exercises to get your creative juices flowing.

It's also the prep work you need to make sure you're in the right mindset to stay focused on your creative work.

In *From Chaos to Creativity*, I point to YA fantasy author Katie Cross as an example of someone who's doing the best to make the most of her time.

In an interview with the folks at the Sci-Fi and Fantasy Marketing Podcast, she said she only has time to write when her toddler goes down for a nap. So for the rest of the morning, she makes sure all her phone calls are made, emails answered, and chores are done by the time she puts the kid down. She eats lunch so her energy levels are good, and walks the dogs so they won't come bugging her during the middle of her writing time.

Don't waste your creative blocks because you don't want to take the time to get yourself set up for success.

Here are some ideas for warmups:

Prep your mindset

Are you feeling frazzled and overwhelmed? Are you feeling rushed? Or are you ready to dive in and do your best work?

Take the time to get your brain in creativity mode. If you're feeling distracted by other tasks, try a brain dumping exercise to clear your brain out. Or if you're feeling anxious, find something to help you transition from anxiety mode to creativity mode.

(I like that Wordle game as a transition. It's an interesting puzzle that gives my brain something to chew on for a few minutes to distract itself from being anxious.)

Prep your work environment

We talked about your physical environment a few weeks back. Before you sit down to work, check to see if everything you need is at hand.

Do you have all your tools? Your reference books? Your notes? Your scissors?

Think about this like *mise en place* in cooking—prepping your ingredients and tools ahead of time, so that when you're cooking a meal you can focus on your craft rather than running around finding everything you need.

Prep your energy

After I had a total pre-dinner meltdown a few months ago, my husband put a note on his phone to remind me to have a snack every afternoon at 3:30.

My brain goes completely into feral panic mode when I'm hungry, which means I can get way more frustrated than usual with easy tasks, my creative work suffers, and I shouldn't have important conversations with my husband.

Learn your body, and take the steps you need to make sure your energy is in the right place when it's time to work.

Prep your ritual

In *The War of Art* (ebook | print), Steven Pressfield writes that he starts his day with the Invocation of the Muse from Homer's Odyssey. But it's not the prayer, or the lucky acorn from the battlefield at Thermopylae, or the lucky hooded sweatshirt he wears that make him have a productive writing day. It's the fact that he has developed a ritual to cue his brain that it's time to write.

Maybe it's a quick few minutes of meditation, maybe you light a candle, maybe you brew yourself a pot of special creative time tea.

Building a ritual at the beginning of your creative time helps cue your brain that it's now or never: it's time for art.

Today's challenge is to not skip the warmup.

No matter how little time you have, set a timer for five minutes and make sure you're in the right place creatively, energetically, and mentally to really make the most of your time.

BONUS 3: SHADOW WORK

When I was creating the first Nanshe Chronicles cover, I spent a solid day trying to figure out a complicated 3D design program called Blender. My goal was to take a 3D model of a spaceship, position it, and render it so I could use it against stock space art to create a cohesive set of covers for my series.

Turns out, this was way more complicated than I thought it'd be.

When I posted in a writer Slack channel I'm a part of, asking for help, a friend responded: "My guide to Blender for writers is hire someone from Upwork."

We joked that he should write a series of guides that all boil down to that single sentence:

Photoshop for Writers, Music Production for Writers, Cover Design for Writers

My friend's point was that I'd spent the day "working," but I was hardly doing my real work.

I felt busy. I was technically being creative. But I wasn't deepening the art I'm called to.

In his book *Turning Pro* (ebook | print), Stephen Pressfield lays out the concept of "shadow careers."

"That shadow career is a metaphor for our real career," he writes. "Its shape is similar, its contours feel tantalizingly the same. **But a shadow career entails no real risk.** If we fail at a shadow career the consequences are meaningless to us."

In other words, artists pursue shadow careers over true work out of fear, and take comfort in the fact that it's *close enough* to what they really want to be doing with their lives.

I've been thinking lately that this concept also applies to our day-to-day work.

Doing real creative work is hard.

- It requires you to sit with the discomfort of not knowing your direction.
- It requires you to sit with the fear that what you are creating won't be well received or isn't any good.
- It requires you to persevere when you're bored, or uninspired, or straight up tired.

It's natural in those times to turn to easier task: *Research, answering emails, talking or reading about your art, tweaking your creativity system, searching for the perfect supplies that will definitely make doing your art easier, scrolling Pinterest or forums for inspiration.*

None of these are necessarily unproductive, and many of them may indeed be a requirement of your art—especially if you're running a business.

But all of those things are shadow work, busywork, shallow work.

None of them take the place of actually doing your Work.

Doing creative work is difficult, and these things are an easy substitute.

But don't let yourself be fooled:

You can't research your way into a completed novel, or Pinterest your way to a finished fashion show. Researching the perfect standing desk won't start your business, and getting to inbox zero isn't going to land you your next gig.

When I found myself struggling with the 3D program Blender again recently, I realized that in part I was turning away from the difficulty or revising my novel.

I was using it as a crutch to avoid deeper, more meaningful work because that work was becoming difficult.

Sure, I did need to finish my book covers, but I also needed to stay with the more difficult Work of my art. I remembered my friend's advice and opened up a freelance marketplace, Upwork.

I hired someone who's passion is 3D modeling, he gave me a 60-minute lesson that saved me a week's worth of struggle, and I went back to my writing.

Busywork is a part of every day. But are you letting yourself be lulled by the "productivity" of it all to the point where you're not doing real work?

I challenge you to pay attention as you work. When do you retreat to shadow work, rather than pushing through the difficulty of real Work?

When you notice yourself making that switch, acknowledge that the real work is hard. Take a break if you need to, then get back to it.

But don't waste your precious creative time and energy on things that only feel like your true work.

Today's prompt: **What part of your creative routine, work, or life is actually shadow work instead of the important work you were put here to do?**

TAKING THOSE FIRST STEPS

I wanted to let you know one thing before I let you go:

You're doing great.

Maybe you made huge changes to your schedule to carve out time for your art over the past week. Maybe you've made a few small tweaks. Maybe you pushed past your fear to say no to one thing in order to say yes to yourself. Maybe you're spending your time more mindfully.

Maybe you skimmed through to the end of this guide and you're planning to go back and do the exercises later —and that's fine, too.

You're doing great.

My goal in creating this workbook was simple: I want to help you focus less on scrambling after some unattainable outcome, and instead enjoy the journey of every day.

Thank you so much for coming on this ride—I hope you'll keep in touch and let me know how your creative reset is going! You can email me at jessie@jessiekwak.com, or find me on the social medias as Jessie Kwak. And I hope you keep experimenting with how you can bring more time for creativity into your life.

Did time tracking work? Awesome. No? Ditch it. Same with blocking out your schedule, bullet journaling, setting a timer—anything and everything I've suggested is only valuable if it's working for you.

If not? Let it go.

There's no silver bullet, there's no "right" way of being a creatively productive person. Let go of what you "should" be doing, and find what feels good to you.

As Madeleine Dore writes in her lovely book, *I Didn't Do the Thing Today: Letting Go of Productivity Guilt* (ebook | print):

"Perhaps we don't want to be more productive in our days, but more *fecund*—that is, more capable of producing new growth, but not always in producing mode. Seen in this light, our days are like fertile gardens: a place to plant, to sow, to weed, to prune, to pick, to compost, depending on the season. A fecund day will look different at different times: some days we did the thing, some days we didn't."

It's so easy to get so caught up in the slog of daily life and a never ending to do list, and forget that we're making progress every day. That we're learning every day. That we're growing and healing and helping—and creating.

Maybe you did some yoga this morning. You picked a healthy side at lunch. You had an epiphany about a plot thing that's been bugging you. You sketched the tree outside your office window. You said no in order to make time for yourself.

Every single one of those things is worthy of celebration.

I'm not saying this like a "rah rah we all get a participation ribbon!" sort of thing. I'm saying that almost every artist I know is ridiculously hard on themselves, and that's a *huge* barrier to creativity—and productivity.

We tend to underestimate or forget the nice things that people say about us, or our accomplishments, and focus purely on the negative. But you can try training yourself to seek out and remember the positive when you make a practice of cataloging your wins.

In that spirit, I'm leaving you with one last assignment:

At the end of every day, set a timer for five minutes and think through your day, listing only the things that went well and ignoring everything else.

Forget about your unfinished to-do list, forget about what you'd hoped to accomplish, and give yourself time to simply appreciate your "win list."

You've got this, you're doing great. :)

Did you enjoy this guide?

Word of mouth is one of the best ways to support authors!

Share your progress on social media, tell your friends about this workbook, and please feel free to reach out and let me know how things are going!

Happy creating,

Jessie Kwak